Slices and Stitches

By

Hillary Kaitlyn Walsh

Intro:

This book is dedicated to all the visionaries, people who are stubborn in the battle for "good", and those who feel they don't "fit". Those elements make a great recipe for leadership and trail blazing. This book is also for those who struggle with mental illness and want to be seen, and regarded as people with important messages to convey. "Thank you" to everyone who taught me about faith, empowerment, and how to build a vibrant life. I'm grateful. My life is full, but full of possibility; hope.

Yes, sometimes I choose words in my writing that will cause the poems to be read and understood in different ways. It is my belief that art is a mirror to the viewer and can have many meanings and interpretations; including what the artist was originally intending to convey. Let my writing be yours *and* mine. Your filter adds new dimension and beauty to my words. I revealed so readers may relate and think, "Yes! I'm not the only one!"

Please read the poems and prose in this book again and again, with fresh lenses from personal experience. You'll learn about my life and hopefully have takeaways for your own. I structured this collection intentionally and it is curated from 11 and-a-half years of experience. There are a lot of people that have been on my mind over the years while writing as I have walked through relationships and situations, but only some poems have specifically one person in mind. Many are written that generalize in order to summarize. I did write a bunch of extra poems at the end to fill in gaps that are more influenced by more recent people I've dated or know, stitched with mischief.

Later in this collection, in the poem titled "The Recovery", I mention fighting "The Battle". It's my term for the mental/emotional struggle of facing the baggage that was given to me by medical staff after my accident about "what to expect", how they believed I was not as intellectually viable as before, and the insecurity I carried about my intelligence and memory capabilities. It took me 9 months to grapple with this until I declared that my brain and memory were "good enough". That declaration ushered in my belief in myself and has changed me in profound ways that I still experience. It was after that that I started to study neuroplasticity and knew I have experienced it myself. I thank God for healing and too many things to list here.

Please watch my Youtube channel for some poetry readings with context (@HillaryKaitlyn). I hope you enjoy my out-of-order poetry and the sorting game with the listed dates by titles at the end. ;) Your uncertainties are my intent. Enjoy!

//

-Hillary Kaitlyn Walsh

\\

"Stretched"

Eleven and a half years of
Legacy, cherry-picked to
show imperfection, rests
in the hopper now. Reform-
-atting and planning the cover
art, I carefully digest the
prospect of being known for
the words and feelings I
cut my teeth on growing up.
Its thrill and chill hit me
like cold air and travel
down
the
vertebrae
of
my
spine.
I bought my ISBN and am
reminded of textbooks and
my college days. These pages
are what I'd put in the liner notes
of my LP. My freshman album. Learning and
bursting told in my punk rock lines, ballads,
sad songs and triumphal entries. My
first try of print. Enjoy!

//

"Visualizing"

I'm finally doing this.
My heart swells, stomach
drops, and an amalgam
of complicated feelings
compete inside. My fingers
gently slip down the pages
and I search for words to
describe the sleek cover.
It is mine, my book of
poems. Finally! Hope
that its stories and snap-
-shots will find kindred spaces
in homes and hearts brings
succor. I don't know the
scale of its success to be,
but don't care because this
baby of many hours and
experiences belongs to *me*.

\\

"Anthem of Twenty-Somethings"

Seasons shutter by
(you can scroll back).
We are laughing and
crying, tired but striving.
Pushing limits in ourselves
and the systems around,
yet finding grit and glory.
Facing choices amongst
the noise. Impossible
to embrace or reject it all.
Falling together or apart,
we coalesce to sift
for shared truths. Downing
cups and finding we *can*
dance in the rain. Some are
peeling off masks. I am
Unmasked, more free than
I thought I would be. I am
a little bent and bruised like
the rest, but fitting to purpose.
Money is not everything. We are.
Discovering what it means to feel
Alive; to give, and to be taken.
Together, we sing and live to breathe.

//

"Maybe"

I think that I
would miss the smirk
that so often plays upon his lips.
I would miss the brown
of his eyes, shirt, and hair.
Taller than me, and strong.
He is a poet, as am I;
though we may be
unevenly matched.
Pale is his skin, which I tease,
and sharp is his wit, with which
I am teased.
He needs to take away
the innuendo,
and some disrespect.
But I enjoy him
mostly as he is.
I am afraid of us ending up
like the others before him:
cast aside and with a bruised friendship.
So I think that maybe,
we should wait.
Or perhaps take it
on a date-to-date basis.

\\

"Caution Sign"

His arrogance, like a caution sign,
makes me proceed slowly.
Bright, big, loud,
it declares a message.
It makes me wonder if
this highway is a good path to choose.
In a few years, when the
workers Humility and
Maturity have left their mark
and the yellow sign is gone,
I wouldn't have to question.
But maybe if the clouds separate
and the sun comes out to play honestly,
smiling, maybe even now I
will drive on.

//

"Not Time Yet"

"Down With Love"!
A movie that awakens within me
the desire to fall in love.
For a long while, I'd had it buried.
Gathering dust, it waited.
But sadly, I know that it's not time yet.
My prince will come when I'm older,
when boys have become full-grown men.

\\

"What's Left?"

You look into the mirror
and what do you see?
Beauty that's only skin deep.
You want to shine- from within.
Take love of Christ, a new way of living.
Outward beauty, like a flower,
soon fades away.
The winds of time blow,
while the soft petals are carried away.
What's left is up to you.
Will I, and you, still be beautiful?

//

"Mema"

Worth more than all the jewels, she stands.
I tread barefoot, and she walks on the sand.
Water laps at my calves
and the air rings with our laughs.
I treasure our long walks,
we always have the best talks.
Just Mema and me,
that's the way I like it to be.
We bake and cook and munch;
there are usually delicious cold-cuts for lunch.
Shopping together, we look.
We may read aloud the latest magazine cookbook.
I never want these good times to end.
Mema is my grandmother and also my friend.

"Happy Weather"

Sunshine falls like rain.
Golden rays beat down:
Sweet, warm, and free.
I want to cry and spin around,
Shout!
Loose and wild, my hair
Flies around me, and
Together, we defy.
Stand still? Never!
Not now, in the bright!

\\

"Heartbeat"

Let your heart
beat like a drum,
quick and deep.
As I smile, I hope
it warms your own sunny face.
When I laugh I pray that
it ripples through you;
light, breezy, mine.
My steps set the
tune of the song of your
heart- for now, at least.
Walk with me awhile,
'til the patterns of my voice
lose their charm and the sound of
my name loses its ring. How long?
Who's to say but God alone?

"...But Not Bitter"

Sun-streaked, pale blue sky
with trailing clouds
looks over piles, high.
Drifts shaped as shrouds,
stark and bright white. Furry
life peers out, quickly
claiming food. Bid hurry
by cold, wet, tickly
snow. We scraped our way again,
yet work remains.
Energy recedes and stirs, train
hour after hour. Restrains
or inspires. Cozy opposite yard
and cut-out trees, inside.
I see painted backdrop ward
shifting. Tonight, again, tied.

//

"Robins' Egg Blue Tea Cups"

Mayan Hot
Chocolate simmers
in my pot.

\\

"Rise"

High skies, so blue, lighten my already
bright mood. I'm smiling, thinking of you.
Someday soon, you will hold me close.
We will laugh and feel so free beneath
another sky like this one. Coming
to a place like that, I'm killing time.
Waiting for you to be mine. But first,
I'm off discovering growth and repair.
It's amazing, how this works. How's
it going for you? Are you rising too?
First thought in my mind: Ocean blue.
Hot sun challenges the beach. Shake
off sand in the water. Dive right in!
Clammy skin and wet suits. Fishes
play and flee. Brighter, brighter!
We will rise again.

//

"Good Day 2"

Pretty sure that today is gonna be a good day,
put a spring in your step and have something
positive to say. Smile rises from the heart,
descends from the mind, and the two make
a perfect match in the middle. Woke up feeling
good, and happy. Don't mind the cold when
Spring's comin'! Spring's fast runnin'!

\\

"Wheeled"

Sit back and flip the pages in this book.
I want to fill it all, but it's exhausting.
Tireless circling thoughts tire me out
these days. By now, I'm looking for new
ideas and any old spoiler. If that day would
just come today or tomorrow, I'd know
what's to become of us. I could rest easy then.
Sleeping's harder when monsters get bolder
in the dark. Dreams that visit are scrambled or
grey; if you only knew what you've done to me.

//

"Words At 17"

Words are easier for me to control, unlike art.
I'm a little clumsy and distracted but oh-so-
focused sometimes. I laugh and I pretend
I'm not deep, but get me alone and maybe
I'll show you the real me. Words are, to me,
a way to reveal truth. Some words lie or are
circumstances glorified, but I try to stay true.
Honesty is golden. Why not vent and breathe
while making a masterpiece? Pieces of my heart
find mirrors in the words I speak or write, and I
find my mind is a dangerous place. This space, in
my head, is freed. Nothing I know I feel, until it
hits the page, is what may spill. There are so many
artists out there like me; my pencil is the brush of
my world, magic carpet ride in a bright sky. Let me
lend some creativity and wait to hear, to see me

change. Awake my mind, and it just keeps going. I rhyme and I hype, and I realize it's best not to fight this. Plug my mind into the page and watch thoughts and feelings flow. It's always an adventure, a journey on an uncharted sea. Scuba divers risk their lives every time, skilled or not. I wonder what I risk. And, what I gain.

\\

"Claiming It"

It's a Sunday and I vow to search for a new person to admire. I'm tired of putting forth so much effort and leaving empty-handed, knowing New Girl will probably be the one to kiss and hold you. For so long I believed I was the one you wanted, deeper than anyone. I was only believing in a lie, my fantasy. I've awoken, and what I see is cruel reality.
I'm so glad that I'm indestructible, and you can't hurt me. This morning I tipped my head to clean my ears, and tears spilled out. I don't know why, but I do know I don't want to call them yours. I refuse to admit I've been naïve and I gave too much away. I broke off too many pieces of my heart to give them to you. I gambled, and I've lost. Winning is magical, unexplainable. My loss stings, but I'm too numb to feel it. Underneath my skin, there's a hole from when you cut my heart out. I can't hurt anymore.

//

"Real"

What does it
mean to be real? No
one can tell me.

\\

"Update"

Every few hours
I check my cell phone.
No texts now.

//

"Time"

Time escapes.
I love every minute!
Good without you.

\\

"Permission"

I will give you
my permission to seize
the day with her.

//

"Drifted"

I drifted away, some time ago. My heart let go of you. When you were all gone, I realized that the change was gradual. Too many knives cut all of our ties. I find there's nothing left to say and I can't prove anything to a deaf and blind crowd. Two seems pretty crowded to me right now. I'm free. My heart is empty after you, but I feel just fine. I didn't miss you, though now I kind of do. Somewhere, miles away in a sweatshirt grey, you are playing guitar and lacrosse. The biggest loss is our friendship, but truthfully all my girls are better these days. I don't miss having aches in my chest from you. I'm glad I drifted. I hope you miss me and someday you will pull me back to you. Closer, next time. Irresistible. Not now, not today.
We both drifted away.

\\

"Pastel"

Easing back into this notebook, 2 weeks later. It's amazing, all that's happened since. My life, my thoughts, my feelings... all changed. Paging through old dreams and fears, I know I've grown. I will always hold onto some naïvete and innocence, but I will be shrewd, too. Picking up lessons and advice from my path like shells along the ocean. I'll keep them.

"Bad"

Insubordinate
children laugh while the
teacher screams.

//

"In Class"

When I sit here
in class I am tired.
It is so warm.

\\

"Maturity"

Self aware,
A person says, "Sorry."
Resolve it!

//

"Thinking"

Thoughts are like smoke; they rise up,
curling and changing, to soon melt away.
Gone, but their presence is not forgotten.
People are like that, too. Spirals that
took up space before retiring to memory.

\\

"National Gallery of Art"

"Bump" and "Bull" are at it again!
Jen is a bull in a china shop and
I am the bump in the night. Laughing,
hot tea in evenings and funny stories
started it all on Berrypick in Columbia.
I was in college, and she helped teach me
how to grow up. Crying in her arms after
harassment happened at work once, and she
first explained to me how my flakiness made
her feel. I woke up to realizing I needed to
change. Walking alongside each other through
pains during those 2 years I rented from her
(my ages 17-19) was just the beginning
of a deep, gracious, and loving friendship.
I don't need as much direction as I used to, but
she is still my mentor, "cool aunt" figure,
"third parent" (I needed more parenting than my
two parents could give me), and friend. I can't
recap it all, but if I were to encapsulate this
relationship, I'd say it's enduring and
irreplaceable. Jen has taught me so much and I
never want to stop giving back. We have rough
patches sometimes but we always work through
them. Gaps in communication are also understood.
Exactly what I need! Family I've chosen myself.
So grateful! To follow her example one day and be
someone's "Jen" is a dream I choose to realize
when it's time.

//

"One Day"

All of me here,
in this one,
precious moment.
It is a legacy
hard-won many
times before. Battles,
lessons, friendly
encounters shaped
my past and memories,
to set the stage for
the woman smiling
now in the spotlight,
taking the mic.
She seeks to
replace the shame
of those gone before
with pride in her
spotless intellect and
clever mouth. She
seeks to restore peace
to ghosts in the past
with hardworking,
honest hands.
She can do it
with wit and charm
and class. Her
predecessors didn't leave
her without tools
or training. Quiet.
the crowd silently waits

to hear her speak.
I want to hear her speak.

\\

"Uncertain Future"

Future, time rushing at my face
Warm, I know, feels cold and out of place.
The map is as readable as an alien language,
A book I can't flip to the last page.
Balmy breezes or icy freezes near,
In God's plan for next year?
The clocks' hands, no time to rest,
Race in a stalemate, an unwinnable quest.
Stop, stop! I'm not ready to choose!
New York, Ohio, Carolinas? Go on a cruise?
Seriously, I'll just wait it out
'Til the air turns again, and clear's the route.
Sometimes I wish I didn't have to-
College? Is it really what I must do?
If I could, I'd fly far away.
Greece, Tuscany, or France; where I'd stay.
Clouds grey above refuse to show light.
Encouragement and hope, what is right?
Simple stuff, like ice cream and friends
Keep me distracted and in mends.
Lost, unclaimed am I to a destination;
Cast-off dreams, no hope for their restoration.
At least whatever happens, it'll be fine;
This future is Yours anyway, not mine.

//

"Frustrated"

Anger and frustration saturate
My face and demeanor are all super ciliate.
I just wanna GO,
But all they say is "NO".
Well, I'll make my own luck...
I will not rot here in my own muck.
I must run and hide,
In no one here next year can I confide.
Probably false, but it sure feels like it.
Any place that feels like the right fit
is shot down in one hot minute.
Stubborn parents pretend to flex
While I tell them what I hope to be next.
How can I live chained to a place,
a person, a lifestyle? No, away I must race...
(Or at least I want to). For now,
I wrestle until my inner adult begins to show.
I hate this tetherball, I just lose.
To take the edge off, I can't even booze.
Temptations rage inside of me;
Things I've denied for all to see.
A human demon rages inside,
Self-destructive as any who've died.
I don't know what to believe,
And myself, sometimes I'd rather leave...
She is truth and lies, a spectacle.
Her shape, we hope, is not a rectangle.
All I can do is strive
To once again find hope, and thrive.

\\

"Always Questions"

Buoy. Carried by waves
of time, it is questions
and unsteady thoughts.
Sunny skies, choppy seas,
elements may come and
go with ease. The mark-
-er rises and falls.
Bigger and smaller in
view, its composition
shifts. Information, disc-
-overing limitations
and what it is to be
human cause illusions
to slip away. Answers
bring change (in theory).
Life is to wrestle in cadence with the
tide. Affected, asking, pushing forward.
To be real, and buoyant.

//

"Rollercoaster Emotions"

Unresolved anger breeds hatred.
Hatred and resentment grow and branch out,
poisoning all that is "good."
Untreated wounds infect and fester;
Painful, smelly, and gross.
Why didn't you give me a reason?
Or we could have at least talked it out.
No, you had to be a coward and make a mess.

You made me board a rollercoaster,
Hurt-sad-over it-sad-angry-hatred-rivalry.
You are poisoning me, ruining me.
One wormy apple ruins a whole barrel.
Congratulations. My barrel is spoiled.
Now, watch out!

\\

"Spin"

Sick and disgusting, I crawl.
Unspeakable filth lies in my heart.
From my pedestal I must fall;
once sweet, I turned very tart.

I hate to claim ungrateful thoughts
and need for deep healing.
I've rejected time-honored oughts
and realized my world's reelings.

Finally knowing what's been
in me feels like a freeing
gulp of fresh air. Poison
cannot keep me from seeing.

//

"Erased"

Our friendships,
Fond thoughts of each other,
Trust,
The pacts that we made

-Gone.
Carried away by the tide...
I guess we were just writing in the sand.
Maybe none of it was meant to be permanent.
Well, now we know
how real we were.
The pain, the anger and malice;
I doubt we can rebuild this castle.
Working together, maybe we could awhile
but soon enough it'd cave
and be erased by the waves again.
Drifting from each other
like the ocean from the shore.
Clams, crabs being swept up in the undertow.
Powerful, strong, impossible to stop.
Yes, everything has changed between us.
There is nothing left, and the ocean rushes past.

\\

"Summer Dreaming"

Somewhere someone coined, "summer love".
Who says it's between two people? Move
that notion out. Replace with a summer
full of individual vendettas and slumber
(sweet and fresh). Nature sings and shines,
and the sun brings out his all. Whines
of, "too hot," are heard everywhere,
silenced by a sticky mother's glare.
Pools fill quickly, like bags of marbles.
Like birds, people on a lark do warble.
Popsicles and fireworks excite,

burgers sustain and s'mores too, at night.
Lazy ways and heavy, sunny rays
bring darkened skin and relaxed days.
Summer is a season for mischief, simple or not...
People go a little crazy when it gets hot.
Spontaneous trips and seaside dips, adventure
past all the summer fantasies in winter. Nurture
your inner child, yet explore adult amenities.
Lying out to toast slowly and finding serenities.
When glorious days begin to fade away,
rigid, civilized English, math, and science stay,
don't forget memories so bright. Remember:
summer will be back, a few months after December.

//

"Tie Dye"

Color squirts and spills
across unadulterated white.
Crevices are left unfilled,
ordinary becomes colors of light.
Veins unlike any others
spider and network, weaving
around and back, over. Lovers
of freedom change common sleeving.

\\

"Glimmering"

Gratitude is shining sunlight on closeted things that felt worn and sore, and remembering that that which was forgotten is better than good; it's more than enough. Gratitude is saying Thank You, but it's also seeing the familiar with new eyes while taking stock. Potential was there all along. Wonder is flecked on the surface, but understood to be soaked throughout. Fresh energy with these re--discoveries adds a deepening of the colors around and a song in the heart. Cleansing occurred. Having bestows the gift of joyful sharing. The search for treasure brings me back here, to what I have. It leads to what I will have with care and hard work. *Leggo!*

//

"July Prayer"

Jesus, teach me
how to love like you,
how to clearly view
this shifting, broken
world. I know there's
nothing new under
the baking hot sun,
and I ask you, what's
to be done? In the midst
of summer fun and fans'
hum my heart turns to
the lives outside these

blue walls, beyond the
verdant trees, bushes
and leaves. What's to
be done? Which part
is mine? I rest now and
wait for sure direction.
Because, you'll show me.
Love.

\\

"Tipping Point"

The sun slips down in a colorful sky
behind cutout trees and whispering leaves
and roosting swallows I cannot see.
Light changes and shadows shift,
reminding me that life goes on.
That there are fresh situations and new
days to come. I thumb through
scenarios and dreams in my mind, but
none seem to rest with reassuring
certainty. Rabid curiosity takes its place.

//

"Directions"

I can't help but ask why
confusion replaces conviction
the more I live. I try
to find direction, but the friction
of dissonant missions and the
addition of new people and information

to situations cause complications free
of certain proclamations,
leaving me more lost than before.
Adulthood is exhaustion and deciding.

\\

"Cascade"

One, two, *three*,
FOUR, five, six,
seven… ten.
My mind, running.
Ten different directions,
taking me nowhere
after all. All this.
All this body needs
is peace. To let the
rest come. Quiet.
My mind circles
and heart races
against speeding,
unsteady thoughts.
I catch myself going
Down. I will not fall!
I will wade through
turbulence and currents
today. Watch it cascade,
'til fever breaks. Lasting.

//

"Yeah"

Energetic,
hyper. Exercising is
my right answer.

\\

"In Brief"

A short list:
stability, and safety,
someone to hold.

//

"Undone"

We were team
in title, but you
took it away.

\\

"Fool"

Hurt and bruised,
lonely and sad, I
feel foolish.

//

"Together"

Anger, pain are
related. Intertwined.

Bitter in taste.

\\

"Grasp"

I wish I knew
which arms are home,
and among which blue
I will adventure.
The sky, my heart,
so open; space for
indeterminate peoples
and places, faith and changes.
I grasp, though, that not to
know is to trust, believing
in Whom God is and what
He will do. I will patiently
wait for revelations and
continue my wandering
contemplation.

//

"Hope"

Hoping, hoped,
hopeless… choosing
hope again.

\\

"Unclear"

Walking through

water, I cannot see
my feet, path.

//

"Self-Protection"

Pushing away:
a way I protect
my heart, self.

\\

"Made"

A kite: made
for adventure, is
risky business.

//

"Kite, My Life"

A kite: made
For adventure, is
Hardy always.

Through storms
That come suddenly
To bright skies.

I realize
Now I am a kite;
Ready for this.

A kite equipped
With unique design,
Buffeted by the wind.

\\

"In Part"

It is possible
to be cautious and
have open arms at
at the very same
time. Being open
to what comes
to play, and yet
not trusting
those things right
away. I think
that that is part
of wisdom: giving
things a chance
and then making
real decisions.

//

"A'brewing"

"It shouldn't be this difficult,"
I think as stubbornness and believing
I'm right brew a strong tea. I'm not
sure how to keep things going if such
miscommunication and frustration are
going to keep happening. We are in

such a strange place of seeming disregard, while resurrecting our friendship from the dead again and again. Distrust is growing and pushing our islands apart while it feels like our bottles thrown out to sea are read without understanding intended meanings. I'm wondering what's to become of us. We don't want to fight but you can't even give me times and outlines so I can plan.
>>>>>>>*Sips tea*<<<<<<<

\\

"Let Go"

Mental illness:
it can swiftly tear
"myself" apart.

//

"Beyond"

Dreary outside,
yet soul is like
a garden, growing.

\\

"Kiss"

I have wanted to know
for so long

what kissing you would be like.
Better than the boy before,
I am sure.
Nice.
Good.
Private and all our own,
the place between our lips.
Our mouths,
warm and caring.
In a relationship or not,
still sweet.
Someday, soon!
As we look at each other, alone,
kiss me.
Kiss me!
Please.

//

"Loving Relief"

To love, its need
rests deep in every heart.
Created to love and be loved. Feed
the fragile self inside and in others. Art
in action, bringing beauty
that can be seen and felt,
creating waves and warmth. Duty-
free, love is a bonus; yet dealt
with intention. To friends, family,
anyone with a rhythmic beat.
Such relief and pleasure amply
known when allowed to love. Feet

free to walk the extra mile, carry
burdens with others, laugh and cry.
Accepted, experience community. Bury
hatchets, learn how to respond to "why".
Listening, giving, confessing. Creating
together. Love is shared, love is sharing.
Arms for hugging, one's own burdens abating,
strength and honor of this loving, wearing.

\\

"Riddle"

Try and think of what you know.
What is it, said to be fast or slow?
Seeds sown burst and grow wise,
a mystery that sees sunsets rise.
Skin wears into lines, wrought
and folded like a cotton dress.
Bringer of joy, and of stress.
Quintessential answer for change,
a measurement of range.
Do you recognize it? Your best
friend and bitter foe. Test
of all, victim of most. Though steady,
the dance needs learning. Ready?

//

"Haiku 3"

Break open the
hopes, dreams you
hold so dear.

"Redlight Haikus 1"

Awesome friends,
lim'ting rest, and
'chieving goals.

\\

"Redlight Haikus 2"

Forced sabbatic-
-al, but ready for it.
Developing me.

//

"Developer"

Catalysts agitate in order to
pull forward a reaction. Changes
unfold. Choosing to reject fears
of confrontation, mediation, and
consternation, bravery takes action.
These agents are needed, integral
to processes that take organisms to
the next level. Ongoing goal:
catalyze positive change.

\\

"S/X"

What I want:
Natural, eloquent
movement. Genuine.

"Arms"

The quiet moments I spend
with you outside, cuddled
up, are satisfying.
Simple things we have
together. Laughing, talking,
eating, resting. Warm and
safe, held and cherished.
I think I have found
a new favorite place.
Maybe we are discovering
a new favorite person
in each other. Even
an hour together is
Enough.
Rich with our easy
connections.

//

"Conundrum"

Drama, I think I need it.
I miss it, miss feeding it.
I don't need it, I need real
relationships with safety,
care, respect. Hard to undo
maladaptation. Difficult
to know what is okay,
normal, and what is not.
I want answers and to stay
focused if that is what I am

supposed to do. Feeling
empty like a drum. Tender
feelings cooled in me but
his eyes still spell Puppy
Love. Confused, I hold
my turbulence close.
Looking forward to
answers. We can't hide.

\\

"Wish List"

Give me a big heart
with reassuring hands.
A sweet romance start
of humor and soul. Fans
of Orioles with brains
and one or two degrees.
Shirts with food stains
and scarred servants' knees.
He will write eloquently to me.
Power behind what he says
and words that mean as he
said. With sunny days
and cloudy ones too, man
will love me through it all.
Passionate and gracious (tan
or pale), patient with my fall-
-s. Trusting and a partner, I
know he's out there somewhere.
Smiling and imperfectly my

future best friend. Unaware!

//

"Is It..?"

What's his name again?
How many first, second,
and even third dates have
I gone on with men whose
names smudge and blur
in my mind with the
pleasantries and sparkless
good thoughts? Positive
impressions with no
romantic feelings to feel.
No racing heart, blushing or
buzzing fingertips. I tried.
Saying yes, showing up,
laughing because I meant
it with a person I enjoy.
The conversation and
food and drink were great.
Well, I wish him the best.
Whatshisname, I hope
you find her soon. She
isn't me. Thanks for all.

\\

"Older, Begin Again"

25, a new age and ever
Deepening plot of my existence.

Discovery. To keep, to sever,
My eyes scan and hands try persistence
to feel the nearby out. Query,
Daydreams and diverse cravings
Mingle like outdoor scents. Weary
Some days, but carefully shaving
Obstacles down and drinking hope.
Propelled to join in community
And peel the layers back. Cope
with others, straining forward. Opportunity
To coach each others' growth;
quiet satisfaction of winning together.
Needs reveal I am alive, loath
Of getting "less than". Faith: tether
To never giving up. Sweaty brow
And gritted teeth beneath smiles
betraying I know to wait. My vow:
I won't give up on me if trials
Will not keep you (pl.) down either.
I hurt, we all hurt. But pain
Is at times, transient. Changing neither
Base needs or the royal deign.

//

"Gripping"

A tightness inside of me
clenches what I have
and squeezes out dis-
-content. What a lemon.
Making bitterness, not
lemonade. My life is

sweeter than this. A
snarl (or several) in my
plans claw at my satis-
-faction. AUGH! In
cartoon form the steam
rises and covers the "Good"
around. Waters I'm under
are murky and dim but
I know if I were honest
(or positive), I'd see what
I have is agreeable, and
"Enough." I can make this set
Sing. Even the caged bird
sings. Hope, tenacity.
It's the only ten I see.

\\

"This Normal"

A yellow and black promotional
pen cuts samples off my heart
and brain and organizes each
Tableau. The wet blood attracts
the light and alerts wolves.
Get at me, sharpen your points
to tear the pages if you thought
you caught your reflection in
my words. I used to care so
much more what people thought
(about anything, and me).
I could scream, I'm so over it.
At least, I try to be. Insecurities

haunt. They whisper I should
make sure everyone sees my
hourglass shape and slender legs
in iPhone frames. Make sure they
think of me as beautiful, with the
made up face I show once a week.
Critical of myself and wanting to
indulge the whispers while reading
and shaping internal beauty and
Distinction. The desire to control
my image and the perception of
Me wars with my heart to live a
flesh and blood life outside of
Glass. Tough battles I'll fight for
Life. Character building in a
different way.

//

"To My Valentine:"

Put your glasses on to
read this. Think of
thoughts I have of you.
A kind and ambitious trove,
hardworking and patient. My
curiosity is piqued, but
there are walls, fie,
for you to scale. What
tender touch your hands must
Give. You have your own
walls, and healing must
from God be giv'n. Loan

me some time, and so will
we investigate, commemorate,
and perhaps discover thrill.
To these ends I talk and wait.

\\

"Conquest"

Walls be threatened,
Hearts risk flight.
Wishes be horses, set, and
Lancet be tied. Light
Break through clouds
With quickened sight, flower
Of beauties become. Sounds
Made of laughter, joy. Our
Secrets shared. Unsure but
Waiting. On time to Skype, I cower.
Hoping. Here goes nothing, "Salut!"

//

"And Retail Therapy"

Parse words unburdened you,
but closed in on my heart. Made
uncertain my hopes. Through
it I doubted you'd stay. You weighed
factors in your many, tricky questions.
Though I supportive, this made you disappoint.
Will we ever clasp hands in love
to create a story for the ages (poignant)?
I'm even doubting if you will move.

The temptation looms for me to go ghost,
but I can't tell which of us would
miss, miss out the most.
I wish I could.

\\

"Post-Skype"

Make me believe
that you are
mine to cleave.
Someone who can
respect and far
attend, above all
I have known.
Are you one to fall
for, full-blown
partnership material?
Crying again. Chances
pile upon. Serial
or temporary? Dances
through my mind
change so fast. Un-
sure. Will I find
a match, or hon,
(again) empty promises?
I hate long dist-
ance. Miss or Mrs.
Hard waiting this is.

//

"Smoke"

Alright, blow out the candle
as you quietly leave.
I'm not sure what I wanted
after all. Unsure if premature
or overdrawn. Confusion
swirled like leaves
in the raucous wind.
Your silence tells me little, but
I decide to allow myself
to begin again.
*His*tory has reached for me,
and another unknown invites
me out. Unsure, half-hearted,
Sad, I agree (with terms).
Temptation whispers, and I
wonder how much more time
will pass before I again see potential.
Was all of it worth it?

\\

"Too Sharp"

There are some days and times where
my words hurt those for whom I care
as if they are blades. Sharp like my wit
when it's cold, and I play at master lit
in my mind while it escapes through my lips.
Ugly. Often I'd better keep silent so whips
with pointy clay don't rip what's been built;
better to stay silent than be plagued by guilt.

I'd rather speak lightly and pull words like feathers
out of the soft pillow of my mind. Letters
spell out curses or blessing. "Bless and do not
curse," are words to live by. I plot
my life better than I do my words, which just
come out from secret places. This book I trust
to open only for me, or those I give it.
The words come from secret holes, or places I visit
too often. Every day's different, especially
when new things happen each day freshly.

//

"Passage"

Purple journal, you
Look like a stranger
Through a haze. Glue
Between us is weak. Hangar
for bad memories of old
frustration, disappointment, loss.
Sorry for leaving you long and cold.
Fingering through, I feel moss
soft and sweet has grown in
me since, over bricks of past.
After your and others' fine pages win
fulfillment, I'll wide cast
for a colorful confidante. Core
my attentions on ones' pages
and clear the path for
future memory walks. New ages.

\\

"Beginning Season Change"

Spring has taken the baton from Winter. She is near, beginning to transform the landscape. Later morning light and longer evenings encourage my hopes and dreaming. Here, warmer breezes turn the leaves and whisper of the fantastic changes to come. The trees, grass, and plants slept deeply and will awake soon, bursting forth in greens and due in a luscious palette of colors. The crocuses offer me chiefly wonder, and I am caught up admiring the depth of each hue. To grow, the seeds slip into the dark ground, die as they sprout new life, and push through the soil. They chance an existence, peeking into the world, and fast begin reaching ever higher. The impending branches and toil of the buds that muscle their way through to extend from the plants, trees, and flowers. Brave, but compelled, from a pent-up place of purpose and mission. Attend the purpose of capturing light in the leaves for sustenance, held to sharing the beauty and the significance of the noun, and the gloved mission of glorifying their Creator. Valiantly reminding the people He created that they, too, are unique, beautiful, cared for. Loved, whether or not they seek solace under a steeple.

//

"Late March"

I am so glad
Springtime has come.
Flowers are here.

"On"

Sometimes church
is just You and me,
on park benches.

\\

"Sunday Morning"

The cool breeze, indicative
of the new beginning of Spring;
premature in January.
Leakin Hall, one of Peabody's
own, lets delicate music escape
over cobblestones, past statues
and tables to my bench.
Birds fly overhead in a light-
bathed sky. It's peaceful here.
There are straggling passerby,
and cars climb past, but only
a young man a ways away
occupies this Mount Vernon park.
It is here that I will bare my soul
to my loving God Who will make
much of me as I give myself, and
my desires, away. "Release,
and embrace Me", I know He says.
I will. I'll taste life full, then life
everlasting. I Spring into relation.

//

"Recovery"

Drawing back the Venetian blinds, I can once again see the snowy courtyard below.
Storied history of this hospital became part of mine. Lying tethered to a *drip, drip,* dripping thing that drew my Chipotle out and would soon prove there was no tear in my diaphragm. Someone died in the street on a cold Friday night. Against clinical odds, her heart, body and mind were born anew. Baptized by tears from blinking eyes in places sprinkled across the globe, and my own. The crucible was hot and cold in ways I never could have expected. To be caught by a net of my work and extensions many bodies deep that fed my family, wrapped me in a blanket and covered me in prayer.
To know mercy and that it was all my fault sliced and stitched me simultaneously. Broken ribs, skull fractures, and the rest could not bring definition like the bruising to my brain and

subsequently, my fragile ego. 9 months of fighting "The Battle," and the shell of terse baggage was left behind in dust. I was finally "Enough".

\\

"Step Down"

Clad in a napkin-thin covering designed to neither grace nor fit, awkwardness writhed and fear rankled. What had I lost and what would I have to work to regain? Salty, bitter tears trailed down my anguished face. Staring at the wall and playing a worried game of "imagine the destination and plan the coordinates" feat--ured images of school, work, and my internship. Apartment, freedom, friends. City streets. The plain walls were a farce. Prison endoskeleton to keep me in and opportunity out. I fought against the binds and waited.

//

"Yet She Smirked"

"Nurse Ratched" drenched her words in sarcasm and the scent of her rotting soul rose from her stocky body. Her eyes were lit with the perverse pleasure that my pain was deserved. I bore a heavy sentence of grief and her lowered expectations at 20. To despise the villain seemed only right in my compromised state and in the echo of my mother's fierce struggle for answers and quality care. It did not go unnoticed by us that Ratched's preference to delegate note typing resulted in incorrect pages siding the right which was left. We sidled the pain of that and the other disappointments that met us daily. To have forgotten days of this time is a gift I wouldn't exchange. To be free again and healthy were my bruised baby bird goals. Takeaway of baggage about "what to expect" became a bonfire that I dance by now. The "medical gospel" died in me, for me. Fueled, I defied and win.

\\

"Sleep Stealer"

Someone said recently
that time is high currency,
but I miss sleep more
and more. Before
it can be mine again
I must finish the bain
of my existence:
homework. Resistance
runs strong, distraction
creates multiplied inaction,
and the clock steals
my dreams and seals
my fate. I'll a fatigued
student be walking intrigued.

//

"Stumble"

Walking home, to a place where time
keeps track of when to go and when
I begin to slip into forgettable dreaming.
My steps begin to slow as my knees
buckle: I don't want to go on. How
can I? No one to love and what do I
have to look forward to? Gasping for
air as tears rise, I push. I go. I walk away
from something that's been so dear. This
time I really don't know. That may have
been all it will ever be. First love burned
me up and now I will let the breezes

scatter me. I will not let myself stumble…

\\

"Wants"

I want to see your smile,
I want to hear your laugh.
But even more than that,
I want you to want me back.

//

"Sky"

There is no darkness
and no light;
I am in the grey
that comes after a starry
night, but before the glory
of a new day. The dawn
is fast approaching and I
can sense the shift, but
I sit under a colorless sky.
It can't be helped that I
wonder why. What's to
happen to me?
Thankfully I barely care.
I'm not hurting, scarcely
wanting, unfeeling. I'm
fine (look like I'm thriving,
but really, just barely surviving).
Blessed, but echoing empty inside.
C'mon, sky, pick a side.

"Not The Same"

I can't love the same. No one, not friends, no people, the same. Not too deep, because maybe my heart's a little more hollow. Nothing to show for all I gave. Human company feels so lacking. Trust is
different, too. Everyone lets others down. Relationship seems empty after learning so much. It's how I feel tonight.

\\

"Present"

Hop, skip, childhood blips in my memory. Drafts beg to sing in my ears, but music clings to the smooth, curving channels. Notes chase their predecessors like playful children, bringing me delight and a calm satisfaction. Seventeen, healthy, and happy. My life is so good. My family is without serious problems, and growing up, nothing was ever really wrong. This past, my present, and all that I've done lays a hopeful foundation for whatever may come.

//

"And So It Goes"

As time flows and we seal the past, I'm beginning to see more and more how we can

simply appreciate each other and all we gave,
Lost, and gained together. I know we're deeper
and more valuable now because of the scars
that bring understanding. It amazes me how
much a part of me you still are, and maybe
always will be. I still influence you too,
perhaps a little more than I know. Now
musical guidance has come full-circle;
Reciprocal.

\\

"Really"

Really, I've been doing so well.
Skies above are starry and bright,
and platonic love has been really
more than just alright.

//

"Semester Start"

Spinning in a frenzy of
thoughts, racing beats and
gasps for air to breathe, I
found myself in an imperfect
storm. Chemical tornado
cast sanity and stability into
question. Finally taken to a doctor
to diagnose, the prognosis
was both a pole to hang onto
and a bitter taste twisting on
my tongue. "It can't be. I'm

not that person. The stories
I've heard about people with
that are not me." Slow adoption
and surprise that the pills
reintroduced me to "calm"
worked together. Coping and
identity changes brought new
transformation. Finding relief.

\\

"Girl-Friends?"

Acceptance, Love, Compassion.
These are the friends I want.
I'd hold them close, If they
were near and I could. I cried
yesterday because I feel like
I haven't been seeing them
Around lately, in faces or hearts of
people I've invested in.
Feeling misunderstood and
under-appreciated. Why
Give one gifts if she won't
use them, or share my
"True" self if she's not
Welcome? What's the point
of a friendship if we can't
dig deep into our pains, hurt
and dreams? If we can't draw
near around shared revelations,
Because a competitive spark
catches the moment or

sensitivity creates your offense?
I didn't know I was so
Alone.

//

"Self-Loathing"

My body is a tomb.
Decay and dismay fester
here. Exhaustion aplomb
while Shame slinks, lest her
presence be noted. Inner
tragedy occurs with
external disappointment.
Pain of this sinner.

\\

"The Clash"

Patterns and rhythms of
falling in step with
petty or naïve expectations
have elicited my growls of
frustration and sadness
while feeling like a puzzle
piece designed for another
fit. In the years of posing,
of searching, gluing and
wriggling for it, I began
to realize that when puzzle
pieces slip naturally into
place, their individual design

and details blur into a collective body and identity becomes group first, piece last. To create a bigger picture together is beautiful, and to harmonize is like song. However, is the puzzle at hand grand enough to give up my search for maximizing potential? My unique cutout and different print tells me to keep looking. This is not my puzzle or place. I can belong and stand out for good. Find a bigger role.

//

"7-9:??"

The weekly meeting begins. Smiling faces and greetings shine while friends drift in. We are crowded around the Word and breaking seals on things contained before. Our phones and Bibles cast light on new or revisited stories, poetry, accounts. Teaching each other and learning together. Angles, nuances, and ideas swirl and impart wisdom. "Nerds", we like

to research and recount.
Reminding one another and
ourselves of what we have
chosen to believe, and the
Trinity, primary colors that are
the basis of everything, feel
brighter again to renew. We evoke
Hope, passion, and appreciation.
Committed to God and this.

\\

"Easter"

Pollen on my shoes,
carried in the tide
as birds whistle and
the sun dips and sighs.
Water laps and burbles,
dogs bark and citizens call.
Ants hurry and climb,
one on my journal stalls.
The trees sit still, with
subtle rustle by gentle breeze.
Spring is here, Jesus is risen,
and I can sit amongst other
new creation. Thorns, a
salamander, many bugs dance
to the sweet symphony of a
breezy April day on the Bay.
Rest, refreshing, promise.
Water snakes, not afraid.

I will wave and glide like
leaves in the pull of the tide,
of changing times and new
understanding of redemption
in His eyes. Life all around,
responsive to His goodness.
His love will ever be what stirs
and beckons me sprout, grow,
and bloom.

//

"Residual"

Weeks later,
I realize I am
Still saying goodbye.

\\

"Christmas Night"

I'm shaking and uncertain,
I realized I didn't want
To feel that way. I reach.
I dare to hope that maybe
he could be what I first
wished. Harder to want
to give any of them a chance,
but I want so much to find
someone. I hate the losing and
I hate saying goodbye.
Praying for an open heart
and feeling much better.

"Behind"

We, the broken.
Pierced by our
transgressions
(real or perceived)
in the tiny closets
we cower in
upstairs, behind
stricken eyes.
Afraid to live
and sorry to
die like this.
This cobbled
together way
of being. Or,
Being shackled
(invisibly)
to broken dreams
and failed attempts.
We are the dreamers
who became listless
when the dreams
never came to be.
Empty handed, we are.
We are the broken.

//

"Sticky"

Guilty!
I point at myself

in the mirror of
my heart.
Drenched in the
guiltiness I create
and what others throw
or spill.
Agonized,
sometimes I feel
tortured
by my own inability
to let things go.
The stress and
echoes of how I
let myself and others
DOWN,
Down,
down
creates a cacophony of
regret, the din not unlike the
dissonance of mess hall
platters and forks bashing.
Waves of my guilt
overtake me.
Prayer and hopefully
soon, a medication. Still
Stuck.

\\

"The Other 'D'"

The slinky devil is
Back.

He takes the place
of Normal
and makes me
Cry! Oh,
I hate myself
and feel sad.
Disappointed
in
my life.
All of it.
The filter is
Wrong,
I know.
Grey and fuzzy,
sparkles abated.
Considering the
Violence
in my mind and the echoes of,
"I can't," "I won't,"
"I'm not up for it,"
in my head.
Silent lips purse.
How long? He will
slink away
unexpectedly,
subtly pulling
the veil
Back.
He will leave
me
to
Recover,

Readjust.
Rejoin.
Not a moment too
Soon.

//

"Drop"

Numb.
The only buzz
is the heat reaching my
face as tears fill my
eyes and I know
I'm caught
(by Sadness). The
grasping for better
was unsuccessful.

\\

"Conditioning"

A memory of pain, and crying in brokenness over my notebook writing about the ghosts of past men, that haunted me and stilted me on new dates, has resurfaced. Walls were high, and I looked down from my tower in questions mixed with wishes and dread. I'm not her anymore. My thoughts are less emotional, and triumphant, I see that through that dark time I turned the ghosts out after I wondered if it were possible. A little more than a year gone by, and I am proud. Wrestling can produce wins I never expected. I want to keep building strength, and winning. No stalking helps.

//

"Really, War Always Necessitates Dire Aid (RWANDA)"

It began many moons ago,
when the African sunsets gave way
to cooler nights. Light homes
hosted friends; eating, drinking
and talking. Tutsi and Hutu
neighbors shared the dark
and a love of their homeland.
The changes ate away incre-
-mentally... Indoctrination by
cold leaders. False teachings
of hate and suspicion.
These changes tore apart
long-standing relationships of
goodwill between comrades.
Things in common and trust were
pulled back, and when the cauldron
of society had been mixed and murky,
motives had confused evil with truth.
Emotions and fear boiled over.
Knives, sharp sticks and tools
stabbed familiars in the back. Pain,
breached confidences, anger.
TERROR. Fields, blood-soaked:
forever to be tainted by bloodshed
and the spill of murderers' cowardice.

Plebeian Hutus of broken promises,
followers who descended into horror.
Though consciences were marred,
killings continued heartlessly
to lessen their sense of wrong.
The scars and tears in the time
and wake of the 100-day
Genocide came with broken
hearts and deep mourning.
A war of this kind is difficult
to handle, with widespread
destruction on many levels
of society, psyche, land.
Political disarray caused
withdrawal of peacekeepers
and resident citizens of countries
unwilling to dirty their hands...
Even as guilt stained and refusal
condemned their supposed honor
and courage. The lack of assumed
responsibility to help, hold out
a hand or pull together assistance
left threats made by the "good"
to insidious Hutu leaders
useless, and turmoil in the hearts
of the few willing to help. They
braved dangerous streets as
drunken killers plotted and prowled,
and little acknowledgement or
encouragement was given by
their peers in America and Europe.
Why did this tragedy go almost

unaddressed by action of those
able to stop it, people who
could turn the tables and restore?
Why were angry and concerned
cries of a Rwandan lobbyist in
Washington, U.N. and Red Cross
activists waved off? Injustice.
Refusal to do the right
thing; an act of cowardice by
detachment. The moral decision
is a harder but worthier path;
justice is rarely convenient.

\\

"At Last"

When the season changes,
and rain re-engages
the cheerless dirt,
sunshine comes to skirt
the clouds. It's this time
that I churn out rhymes
about the green around
to the sweet sounds
of bands, birds,
and I read and write words.
In the green, sleek grass
my feet wiggle at last.

//

"Favorite"

Weather is a fun expression,
a painfully honest lesson
that the earth, like a person
is always changing: peaceful,
sunny awhile,
or seasonally a turnstile.
If coaxed to pick a favorite,
I'd say, "What am I like
today?" My body finds a kindred
in what's winded or bright,
still and restful or watery in sight.

\\

"Stay"

Time rushes like a bug
to a porch light outside
the banging screen door.
I don't know if I should
wish for more or give in
to the whooshing sounds
past my ears and hair.
Time flies like a bird
in the air towards the
horizon line. Golden rays
shine like the future that
is mine. I look at the clocks
that remind Time is like
fine sand in an hourglass.
I have no idea how long

it will last, but what I do
know is, Time goes by fast.

//

"Channeling"

Bright colors and graphics
crouch with pictures of
lives real or imagined.
Viewers are unconsciously
training to become art critics;
increasingly cynical of
relationships, opinions and
a host of other things in
the visual queue. Scrolling
or trolling for stories to
repackage in gossip, or
seeking affirmation and
entertainment. Time clicked
away reaps a wide variety
of emotions and reactions
to push down since the
escape didn't work. There
are no ropes on the screen
and thoughts may come
clear when not cloyed by
so many competing pieces.
I am avoiding, and finding peace.

\\

"White-gloved"

Veiled in unanswered questions, some things in my past gather dust. Or have only been illuminated to a privileged few. It's not dishonesty, but what was preserved retained with a touch of mystery when considered through anyone else's secondhand lens. I have regard for the price and the payout of privacy. There's something sacred about unpublished details, or un-photographed, un-filtered cameos. Glimpses into vulnerable or intimate or argumentative moments. To slice through my truth and tip my hand to show past times while concealing names and places make me feel like a magician. Care--fully concealing while reveal--ing. Taking power back.

//

"1517"

I made him premium in
my schedule, planning
around his whims. Waiting
until the last minute to invite
me, he'd twirl me around
his pale fingers. Strawberry
blond and cute, but cold-hearted.
I swallowed his disregard because
it was how I'd been trained before.
I made him a gift and he only
planned on hanging it when he
found it fit to pretend we could
become something. I knew the
first night we reconnected after
the nights we drank in an inter-
-national crew that we could
never clasp on a title and swim
together. Different kinds of fish.
We wanted to be wanted, less alone.
It was only a game of keep away
and so many things made me feel
crazy. Trying to balance the scales
was rejected. I boiled. Began change.

\\

"Click, Click"

If he felt like a fool, I'd have succeeded. It wasn't much after it ended that I needed. Makeup in place, clothes fit to face, I want to be seen. I'll laugh and

be a full-color presence, no longer an echo of the vibrance I used to have. It's in the rhythm of relationships, part of the up after the down. The part where I admit I'd rather drown in almost any new ocean than his, but he can drown in mine. Best if he regrets what he didn't do as I move on.
Ssssss, it burns.

//

"Unhooked"

It was radio silence strung
between us, unmoved by
whichever storms were passing
through each other's lives.
I wouldn't know, nor would you.
We don't keep up (we only kept
up with a goal which we threw
away through careless busy-
-ness). We are ripples on each
others' feeds on the cycling
net and apps. Time dims the
color of the memories, but
it is with clarity that I say,
Were it meant to be then we
Would still be. Waved on.

\\

"Come Back Soon"

Biting my lip and pricked
eyes wet my senses. I

miss you. A world away,
but not so far we can't
WhatsApp. Soon we will
touch again, and again.
Rhythmically, passionately.
I'll feel you completely
(as much as I can now,
in the beginning). And
I'll draw you down deep.
It's me, and it's for you.
Off to a good start.
I hope we can keep
adventuring, together.
Laughing, resting, dancing.
Celebrated and smiling.

//

"Slow Motion"

The dreamy waves recede
when my eyes slide open.
Mr. Sandman left some granules
behind but the day is NEW.
Light streams in through
windows like a searchlight,
finding me and binding me
to accepting the challenge of
Today. What to discover,
who to see. Whom to be.
So alive, and so much
ahead of me in this one day.

"Turning"

Feeling underestimated and at a loss. How do I begin again? My heart geared up and was let down. Taking a break was what I needed but I want to find again, try again. The repetition of the search has proven that though details be different, outcomes run the same. How tired of the circus wheel turns and swinging from right to left. I lament the process and the sigh of excitement cum break-
-down. When will it end? When can I find my Home?

\\

"Mazed"

Weary body causes the mind to overpopulate its channels (exasperation ensues). A headache comes to underline my <u>desire to sleep</u>, but a weakening of powers bungle progress. Discomfiting thoughts of Today niggle and the echoes of noise from speech and cars compound to form a tapestry that lace me in. Knowing to angle toward completing my routines (believing climbing into bed will help), I trudge on. Quiet (and dream-filled sleep that may bring Rest) wait sparkling (but gracefully) in the wings. When I turn out the light, my monsters may fade, too. A heavy slumber, I hope, until the morrow. Zzzz

//

"Subtle Feels"

A quiet whisper inside me like a gentle rustling of leaves stir a desire to love and be loved, for Companionship and Adoration. The thrill of a consistent person who still excites the heart and mind after stretched time. Someone to call "Mine" is somewhere out there. My heart silently calls him. Mystery, man.

\\

"Premium"

Wrapped in a chenille blanket,
I soak up the stillness
of an unexpected afternoon
Home. Golden light filters
through the undressed trees
in the woods. Gradation
I can watch through the window
Before it leaves. A reprieve
from speech, an arrest from
answering aloud. Savoring.
Unscheduled, uncommitted
Time is a welcome guest.
Recuperating and warming
my thoughts alone. Better
To share once processed
Before. Impressions take shape.

//

"January Flakes"

I stepped out into the still fullness. Cray Pas navy reminded me of the soft, full-size flannel sheets that soak up sound. The best thing about them is they don't get cold in a made bed like cotton sheets do. *The sky felt even more dense as all of those descriptions strung together. It continues.* Being out there, walking on my tip toes on the cotton-soft snow, I felt privy to the reveal that the hyped-up snow was nothing more than hopes of sleeping in and children's reason for the snow dance. It was not an inch and a half. Cold irony pricked my face and I soaked in the blues and blacks. The stinging white stopped before I trudged back. Roads fine. 9:20 alarm, we are a GO.

\\

"The One Who Got Away"

He showed up on my daily list.
I "liked" and he liked me
back. Finding so much in common,
we messaged back quickly. Easily.
Met sooner than planned because
we didn't want to wait. Nerves
that proved to lead to something
beautiful. The night shimmered
like a dream. Federal Hill Park
overlooked a painted tableau
of lights and undiscovered stories.
We stayed longer than we planned,
lulled by the magic to keep our
hands clasped together and mine
treasure in each other's auras.
It was the beginning of something
brief and memorable. We couldn't
pass the test of time or his trip,
but I let him get away so he could
be whole. The hole he left
Will be filled one day by new
magic, the kind with the
power to stay without "settling."

"Summer Flung"

He was a brief, shining star
in my life. An unbridled
surprise, a pulsing ball
of energy and life. We
found each other beautiful
and planted compliments
like kisses on cheeks, quick
and sweet. To hold his hand,
wish to encircle his heart
were intermingled with
smiles in my daydreams.
Feeling like we'd known
each other longer and building
a plane to make it so couldn't
save us from the wreck.
Brokenness that caught up
with him when in Europe
he tried to escape his world.
I lost him there but I hope he
finds himself: shining bright.

//

"Yet"

My heart has been
Split. Romantically in
stasis, and otherwise
growing and thriving.
Full with love for
friends and clients.

One day I'll find one
to get excited about,
a man to love. Maybe
just not yet. Accepted.

\\

"Recently Self-Directed"

"When it rains, it pours," They say.
It's a perfect storm of early mornings
and fun called "work". A little sick
of driving, but it's probably because
my body's adjusting to less sleep,
more activity. My Fitbit is coaching
me to push myself and I strategically
am not addicting to coffee or tea.
Long days, but it feels like doing
life with a few special people.
Supporting each creating their own
"best life". Happy people, more
complete families. Thanks, Maryland!
Enabled, not disabled. Grateful and full.

//

"Contracting Works"

In a flurry of activity,
the feelings inside change
many times, but I can
choose. Must decide to put
the other first and to be
patient. Flexible to

weather, moods, and their
money. Entertainment abounds
with education, exercise,
radio singing and quality
time. I read aloud. We talk,
laugh, and play. Let's keep
choosing hours discovering
and learning with each other.

\\

"Still Awake"

It was a quick sunset,
though I guess its
buildup was gradual
and quiet. Punchy pastels
streaked quickly and
large color blocks turned
a pale blue. You told me
you buy things to make
me happy and care for
you, but that isn't what I've
wanted. Gifts last, but
sweet smiles, hugs,
time in person; gentle
words and touches are
at the top of my wishlist.
We compared the currency
of our words and actions.
Each shared what was meant.
Misunderstandings, miscommunication,
perennial expectations of

how the other person
might be over text.
We pushed aside cobwebs
and shone flashlights on
hidden things. Revealing
aches and confusion, we
considered our struggles
with trust. A crossroads.
We chose the left, by water.
A second first date and a
pact to be honest, clearly
communicate, and trust.
Doubts still linger, but they
have joined the conversation.
Progress was not forgotten.
Long-term or just a little
longer, we shall see. We.

//

"Ajar"

"Santa is not real,
the Easter Bunny isn't
either," a young me took.
I stopped believing.
Belief. Puts a
spring in my step
and a song in my heart.
To watch it ebb away
and sometimes go is
sad. Shutting a door and
the light is gone.

Will my belief in us
come through the door
again, get on track?
I'm not sure if it was
built to last. Belief,
will you come back?

\\

"Sugar Rot"

When things are more
than an arms' length
away, they are sweet
like candy, salted like
caramel. Craved and I,
craven, only when the
far away gets close.
Suddenly shaking, not
from anything but an
expectation of sugar rush.
A lie, it's more than that.
Doubts and fears with
concern to time and being
ready. Heart racing,
things to tidy and pack,
thoughts and situations
to UNpack. Heavy.
Gnashing my sweet teeth.

//

"In Grades"

Pressurized colors
BURST and flew like
fireworks from a can.
The only pieces missing
were the stertorous sounds.
I drove home with
the dawn. She adjusted
tones and showed me
what had been lying
in shadow. Broken Bells
were blinging and I considered
stories. What is ours,
here? What is mine?
Colors traded and I
found myself back
in Kettle's queendom.
She rubbed the car
Welcome. No longer
night, but morning.
Can the dawn of a new
day bring a fresh start?
I need refreshment of
Everything. And more
hope. I am not Lost.

\\

"Showered"

Suds encircle golden
hair as lace crowns
precious things.
SPF 50 and sweat
from a full day are
cut with minty soap.
A refresh button is
pressed in a bare
room along the maze
in an impossible to
reach tower. Captive
princess remembered
the secret of being
Free. The choice:
use it or risk
Everything.
Rediscovering
her worth and
recognizing her
beauty were part
of a new wave
that brought a
smile. Clean again.

//

"Life After"

I jumped ship, knowing
the water couldn't be colder.
Started swimming and diving,

Seeking. Sometimes, hiding. Bolder
in theory than I felt or
Lived. Testing and guarding
Faith that there is for
Me something "good" regarding
Work. Stepping into paid roles while
My passion and heart wait at home.
Still searching, echoes style
their ways back. Dreams roam
to touch others' pain and bring
Hope and invitation to a new
Story. Colorful places sing
as I bend the bars; true,
I pick at the locks. Kept
yet free. God is my Keeper, so
is me. Perspective: become adept
at riding out changes. Become, do.

\\

"Bad News"

My heart races with the end
hours out of sight. How easily
I forget, articles and videos
political in nature stir and pull
anxiety from me. Distress and
Worry that I am powerless
to help and trapped in a choice
between a sand pit or slackjaw
Fear of watching a disaster unfold.
Pulling on my methods to cope
and stuffing the Crazy down,

I'm revealing only minimum
Concern while screaming inside
me only. It helps to know that
eventually this will pass.
I'll make sure I vote, sign petitions.
Honestly, right now I only want a donut.
Distraction and relief. Forget to
Reset.

//

"W17"

Winter sweeps in, a draft through the window. Cold fingers touch my face and spread a chilly blanket over the space. As the sky turns milky-white and prepares snow, I know it's the beginning of seasonal things. Sleigh ride adventure of fun or full of bumps and skids on ice. There might be laughter and falling together with whomever it is in my wintry mix. I consider and I resist turning on the heat. I can withstand cold and whatever this season brings my way. Pulling a blanket of my own choosing tight, I am layered like a cake. Colorful and ready. I settle in for my book and the curious ride.

\\

"Ha"

Each Ex has asked in my
daydreams, "What do
you think of me?" It
is met by my grimace.
"Do you really want to
Know? Wait, how do you
mean that?" Weighing
the options before me.
Incomplete answer or
destruction by dynamite?
The need to tell him
what I think bears heavily
and always at the expense
of his pride. If it's whom
he showed me he was or
how he neglected things
with me it's not my fault
if one externality is a
damaged ego. Because,
Damn. He deserves to
know if he was one who
did hurt me. Don't hurt the next
ones. We can both
feel some pain in the
END.

//

"Shiver"

Sometimes I wish I
had Never met him. He's
so flaky once he loses
focus that he doesn't ever
follow his good intentions
through. I am left holding
the gifts and other secrets,
like poems he's never read.
My things gather dust in a box.
Doe-eyed and dapper,
tramping the earth to find
a nameless thing. Always
looking, thinking he has
found something that Shines.
Rapt before it loses its sheen.
Why did I have to find him
and shimmer before blunting?
Glad I knew months ago that
it was over when it was done.
Yes, Thank God. There will
be another; healthy and happy.

\\

"Reflection"

I want to love you
like we've never loved
Before. Before, we were
mismatched. Today,
made anew. The heart

in me can't feel you
through the walls of
past and though the mind
sees what you do and
how you take care. Our
friendship is best desc-
-ribed as close, dear.
We laugh at jokes we
quickly recognize and
harmonize. You say,
"Wait and see." I say
Hmm, to me. Agree?

//

"Even Again"

Lavender chamomile tea
warmth pulls the edge
off the cold. Here again,
in the place where I wait
for your mood to shift
Again. I wish you
could separate thought
from feeling like I can.
Moments come where my
heart grows soft and eyes
fill and prick with over-
whelmed caring. Take
the moment and hold it
tight. I release it like a hug
and emotions abate. Calm
and even again. Looking

forward to you even again.

\\

"Into Me You See"

Another Christmas is coming and
I am untethered and unattracted.
The calm within me languishes
and my shrug comes with an
apathetic >sigh<. I can hold myself
(arms to body and self to goals)
For a love without strings or
conditions.

The standards I have been
curating in my mind stack
high and frown at the parade
in front of me. But, the one
I want to want I can have
and I do have but we
cannot break the glass ceiling
in front of us to grasp at
romantic love for each other.

For all our depth and companion-
-ship, Friendship is the craft we
cannot climb off. Anchored in
unfamiliar friendlationship
territory, the sun beats down
and we scratch our heads.

Not yet? Will it happen to us?
We wish but don't know if

it can ever be. It didn't
work before (when we
choked on our pains).
Other ships may be coming
for us and changing our
coordinates to each other.
Holding, we wait.

//

"Out of Sync"

I know you collect dead presidents,
the kind you can crinkle in your hand
and spend, but I also know what else
you collect. Even though I'm not the greatest
at remembering what you've said, I know
who you are, what you like, and what you're like.
It's difficult when we're both down, sad, or
frustrated.
We go throat to throat instead of back to back,
forgetting we're on the same team.
It's easy to dislike each other when
the compassion, heart, and patience
aren't there. We're distrusting, and as a team,
we fall apart. The lack of romance is so utter,
you could be the brother I fought against
as a kid. I'm glad we know how to
set our misunderstandings aside and
shake hands to end the match.
We only win if we're fighting together.
Reconciliation refreshes.

"Kckrrksssk"

Together we are safe.
The world of deceit and
smoldering pride places
landmines in common
spaces. It cloaks much
meaning under words and
bedroom eyes (that are
intended only for a night,
but seem to promise more).
Spending a year burning
our own trail has made
something solid, secure.
Hard-won, our friendship
rose like a phoenix out of
bruises and cuts from others
before, and pain we brought
each other. To have made
it this far and through our
iterations, we have kept on.
We are stronger. Better ind-
-ividuals and as a unit. Fire
in candles crackle as we
text apart to celebrate our
upswing and agree: Keep On.

\\

"Shake My Head"

"Too nice" turned into me falling
on my own bottle opener. Before,

it's been drawing my arms so wide
I've tripped myself when they
caught another's glance. Or, given
so many quality gifts the chase became
"too" predictable and the healthy,
mature relationship I offered was
not dramatic "enough". I've gone
through my share of valleys and
peaks. Sometimes, I've set traps
for myself. Thinking I was going
to set a record for "Best", I was
pushed away instead of to the
top of their list. My gifts and
compliments filled my hands,
arms, but left my company
empty after all. I go through
this, change my tack, and often
the cycle is repeated. Loving,
caring "too much", "too" well,
"too" anything. I wring my hands.
Perhaps the lesson is finally
becoming clear. If I am healthy,
my build is to give. If others are
unhealthy, they chafe at the "scary"
and unconditional love. Rather
than feel threatened by uncharted
territory or deep waters, hitchhiking
with a stranger takes preference.
Maintain your slow fade with an
emotionless mask. I'll keep your
insecurity and fear as my regret.

//

"Sightline"

Hindsight is 20/20, but
Looking Back, it is possible
to see that there was no way
to have known. Awareness and
careful sifting of words and
actions and writing it all
down does not always flag the
person or situation. It's okay
to have invested time and energy
into something that was only
fool's gold. It didn't make me
wrong, only a little more wise.
To tend a garden with plants that
die is not to be empty-handed.
It produces patience and teaches
to let go. Tilling enriches dirt
for future growth. The garden
was beautiful. I collect invisible fruit.

\\

"Ash Blows Away"

A long stroll down a twilit path
is the last step of processing
before releasing bad memories
of people or things into the night.
Writing leaves a receipt and makes
something physical out of invisible
spiderwebs. Burning the papers in
my Mexican fire pit with incense

while praying and listening to a song
on repeat was meditative. My heart
released its bitterness and
disappointment about the job and the
sinking ship it felt a part of. Baggage
went up in flames and was traded for
catharsis. Sometimes a fragrant candle
casts shadows of dancing fire nymphs
in a dim room while I journal and tell
God what's amiss, and what I think I
need. These quiet moments are necessary
to do important, internal work. Spring
cleaning clears the way for new.
Old walls acquiesce to new growth.

//

"Dried Up"

I pressed you in the pages, layers of my heart.
Your color has since dimmed, but I'll never forget.
Frozen in time, your shape is kept yet fragile now.
Your strength and muscles flattened here and your
reach is weak. To touch this form risks it breaking.
My warmth and shape are your opposites and keep
us further apart than we ever could have been
Before. Decreased yet continuing to exist, you are
flowered, fading memories. A far cry from whom
you were, but you are and will be past.

\\

"Precious Memory"

Sometimes when I let my mind
slow down, I imagine a dreamy
scape where I return to the image
of a silken, full flower. It's in my
arms, and is slowly opening.
I was 17, and it was the image in
my mind when I thought about
Love. I was grappling with how
to tell my first love how I adored
him, and I was thinking about how
much I felt already. Searching for more words to
make lyrics he could use in a song, and feeling
bubbles rise like ginger ale. A quiet knowing
in my heart painted me this picture
and I knew that whatever I felt then
was like a rich budding, to be eclipsed.
One day I will love bigger, deeper.
My heart will bloom in lively fullness.
To love like that, and to know petals
will continue to open, becoming even
more beautiful, is a promise I hold
close when there is no potential
shimmering in front of me. It is
a compass, directing me to "Keep
Looking". It takes time to see if any
interest will be to tend and sprout
into feelings, but this vision helps me
to be honest with myself. I stop,
gauge, and choose to keep moving on.
Someday my search will end.

I'll look internally and see
my heart becoming so.

//

"First Impressions Upgraded"

You call me on the phone. I know you well from the past, and we've kept up. These girls, they aren't treating you well (from the first to the last). As your friend we catch dinner, a drink or a movie. I tell you after your breakups (and ups and downs), you'll find better; you'll find her. I hope you stop dating the same archetype of females that don't know what they want, then after stringing you along, they aren't ready for a relationship. They threaten to sink your battleship, but you never go down without a fight. To have watched you grow these past 5 years has been gold. You deserve great things, man. We get along better than ever now but I'm glad we can "Cheers" and cheer each other on, in separate arenas. Recount refereeing and red cards. Stay in my life and let it be just like this. I'll "let you" beat me in Sake Bomb. Or maybe I'll beat you next time.

\\

"Forward Motion"

Dancing is a common theme in my understanding of the give and take of love and life, excitement and let down. It's also a pastime that I used to fear, besides a handful of special memories of dances to songs on the car stereo, then smartphones, with beaux. Other good memories of dance were salsa lessons a few times, at Latin Palace and a surprise party. Dancing is an invitation to risk embarrassment and learn. Generously, someone said I was, "made to dance." Heels I brought to attempt helped me climb into grace that I didn't think I'd have. The compliment glowed in my jar heart and gave me hope to light the way. Learning, I move forward more than back to a new song.

//

"Forward Motion Too"

Some songs and bands feel ruined by associations but I like to rebel against the feeling by listening despite, trying to appreciate them anyway.
For me, I do. Vinyl and mp3, radio and playing in my head, I will still appreciate the songs without because they were always catchy.
The musics' grip never let go.

\\

"Hands Up"

Reading back through and writing to express my truth, many of the past pains have lost the names and faces of those who caused them. Too many people were "too busy" to

maintain a friendship that I
honestly can't remember or
carry a grudge. I gave up competing
for a spot in their schedule. Maybe there was
more I could have done. Busy society
and shifting, nebulous priorities have created
a beast I guard against and cannot trust.
Providing RSVPs other than "Maybe" are
struggle for me, too. I'm hoping
we can walk through this shake-
-down socially and be alright.
Just remember, I want to see you
or hear from you about my party,
and you won't draw my scorn or
lose a friendship if you can't come.
There's always next time.
Let's take the chance for a next time.
Maintaining friendships is hard;
starting fresh again, and reconnecting, warms.

//

"Technicolor"

Dreaming out loud is like a child blowing bubbles. Spinning around and seeing hopes rise; some latching to each other and popping, with laughter. Greens and blues seem captured for a moment and look even better with a rainbow sheen. To laugh and believe that somehow these circles and oblong shapes are portals to see into other dimensions. That magic *does* exist. Childhood wonder wasn't lost back then. Excitement expands in beauty.

Delight, and with high spirits, reach for the sky;
Float Away.

\\

"Design"

Night owls are wind up dolls that open glass eyes slowly, lashes heavy. Wooden movements pick up the pace as the day passes by. Feet snap to attention as the sun dips and trades places with the moon (after bright colors fade into dark). Early birds are wound while they sleep and begin moving when the sun punches in for its shift, or before, for the earliest risers. To run the dollhouses and other cutaway structures and transportation, the rise and fall of energy must balance, like clockwork. Night birds hem and haw, but common work and schedules must live and die by daytime hours in order for forces to meet in the middle of the afternoon, everyone's half-mast. Niche work fits the extreme. Daytime tasks are working, but my favorite is firing on all cylinders at night. Creating, exercising, etc. It's a hoot!

//

"Impetus"

Elusive is as mysterious does. Reflecting on how understanding how to create safe spaces eluded me while I was "crazy" and how the mystery of finding enduring sanity has taught me so much. Experience and perspective grew. Internal noise was quieted enough that I listened, read, and learned from external sources.

Episodes of "crazy" are not an everyday affliction to me, and they are so rare now, but growing up with this brain gives me insight and compassion for how to create that which I could not understand before. Freeze the thought or feelings; back up, study. Consider the source, and what would happen by mentally following breadcrumbs the decisions would leave. My heart has grown many times since the memories I covered with shame like sheets on furniture. Studying my mistakes with honesty and a constructive eye have helped me see what I couldn't understand or get right. The dust twirls in the sunlight hitting the scene, and I know it's confetti to celebrate my new truth, today. Progress (a long way). I send silent apologies to those who felt encumbered by the perfectionism I choked on and built into a lattice with which I taught and asked for specific, multi-tiered answers. It was 19, when in the downs I walked through a cloud of self-hate and dissatisfaction. I thought expectations were the ladder and not the one who pushes the ladder off. Breaking that bus windshield at 20 was one of my best worst mistakes. An overhaul I never saw coming. It took time, and I'm not done metamorphosing, but now I am known for being safe and responsible. I'm sorry for the past, proud of the present, and building to continue protecting people and the future. The skeletons in my closet linger and spook, but they are fuel to my fire; I will not stop. There's so much hope, love, and healing to be an integral part of. My heart cries, "Let me be there!" I am, I will.

\\

"Ahhhhh"

Breathe In, deeply.
Out, slowly. Thoughts
grey and Time slows.

Flipping the script on hot air. A wind that cleanses and refuses to stir things up. This ex- -ercise is good for every one. Beginner level that strips away barriers of age, background and ability. It is true Democracy. Ahhhh

//

"Reverse-Engineer"

I like the problem solvers and doers. People who say, "This isn't right," or, "I don't like this," and find ways to make things work, or work better. I think it's easy to complain and say you don't like something before letting it be, but that is its own kind of cowardice. Creativity is one of the best things to have; it adds notes in the margins that make new connections, designs the secret sauce for success, and makes life sing. When making a team, or finding people to fly with, imagination and vision (for more, better, cohesion) are prerequisites for me. Don't spend a lot of time complaining about things you're unwilling to influence to change (a conscious adjustment worth making). Those who make a difference are the same ones who pushed the boundaries and sought out to see what they couldn't do. Red tape has a penchant of falling away.

"Naturally"

The surface of the water is dappled by sunlight and offers only a limited view of the shadows underneath that pass like ships in the night. Detritus of the biome disturbs the superficial body and float briefly before slipping into the dark archive. Strangely, the movements and sounds here don't comfort or cheer most days like they worry, overwhelm, or stress. It's in this reflection that I see how it is I want to face this. A strong fish, propelled upward, breaks the surface to sail in the air and once again slip under. To post, revel and connect, then return to my mysterious, un-photographed life. Private, quiet moments are gold. Yes. The light will filter down on me here. I'll wait for when I'm ready, because I don't need steady hits of the noise or overstimulation of information. Relationships can sneak behind the pages and friendships thrive under the radars. Soon the moments of giving and sharing will sparkle in the sun before descending out of sight.

\\

Dates of Poems And Prose:

"Stretched" 1-09-18

"Visualizing" 12-31-17

"Anthem of Twenty-Somethings" 8-29-17

"Maybe" 3-20-07

"Caution Sign" 3-20-07

"Not Time Yet" 4-03-07

"What's Left?" 5-06-07

"Mema" 12-20-07

"Happy Weather" 5-24-08

"Heartbeat" 5-06-08

"...But Not Bitter" 1-24-16

"Robins' Egg Blue Tea Cups" 1-18-18

"Rise" 3-10-09

"Good Day 2" 3-10-09

"Wheeled" 12-28-08

"Words At 17" 1-13-09

"Claiming It" 12-07-08

"Real" 2-10-09

"Update" 2-13-09

"Time" 2-10-09

"Permission" 2-10-09

"Drifted" 2-26-09

"Pastel" 2-26-09

"Bad" 2-13-09

"In Class" 2-13-09

"Maturity" 1-10-18

"Thinking" 6-19-09

"National Gallery of Art" 1-14-18

"One Day" 2-08-10

"Uncertain Future" 11-13-08

"Frustrated" 11-16-08

"Always Questions" 3-04-16

"Rollercoaster Emotions" 2-27-07

"Spin" 7-04-10

"Erased" 3-04-07

"Summer Dreaming" 11-20-08

"Tie Dye" 7-09-10

"Glimmering" 1-18-18

"July Prayer" 7-27-11

"Tipping Point" 7-18-10

"Directions" 7-11-10

"Cascade" 1-11-16

"Yeah" 11-19-14

"In Brief" 12-05-14

"Undone" 12-05-14

"Fool" 12-05-14

"Together" 12-05-14

"Grasp" 3-11-11

"Hope" 12-05-14

"Unclear" 12-05-14

"Self-Protection" 12-05-14

"Made" 12-17-14

"Kite, My Life" 12-17-14

"In Part" 1-19-15

"A'brewing" 1-14-18

"Let Go" 1-23-15

"Beyond" 11-17-14

"Kiss" 3-21-07

"Loving Relief" 2-23-15

"Riddle" 12-18-15

"Haiku 3" 1-27-09

"Redlight Haikus 1" 8-07-15

"Redlight Haikus 2" 8-07-15

"Developer" 1-06-18

"S/X" 4-24-16

"Arms" 6/03/16

"Conundrum" 7-07-16

"Wish List" 7-25-16

"Is It..?" 12-26-17

"Older, Begin Again" 11-06-16

"Gripping" 12-18-17

"This Normal" 12-18-17

"To My Valentine:" 1-31-16

"Conquest" 1-31-16

"And Retail Therapy" 1-17-16

"Post-Skype" 3-23-16

"Smoke" 3-01-16

"Too Sharp" 1-13-09

"Passage" 6-04-17

"Beginning Season Change", 3-29-14

"Late March" 3-25-12

"On" 1-08-12

"Sunday Morning" 1-08-12

"Recovery" 1-02-18

"Step Down" 1-03-18

"Yet She Smirked" 1-03-18

"Sleep Stealer" 11-27-10

"Stumble" 3-25-09

"Wants" 3-23-09

"Sky" 9-15-09

"Not The Same" 3-25-09

"Present" 4-02-09

"And So It Goes" 5-18-09

"Really" 4-25-09

"Semester Start" 1-03-18

"Girl-Friends?" 12-18-17

"Self-Loathing" 9-21-16

"The Clash" 1-03-18

"7-9:??" 1-02-18

"Easter" 4-24-11

"Residual" 12-11-16

"Christmas Night" 12-25-16

"Behind" 6-27-17

"Sticky" 6-25-17

"The Other 'D'" 6-16-17

"Drop" 6-16-17

"Conditioning" 1-18-18

"Really, War Always Necessitates Dire Aid (RWANDA)"
4-28-10 *For a school project*

"At Last" 4-03-10

"Favorite" 3-28-10

"Stay" 5-01-10

"Channeling" 12-22-17

"White-gloved" 1-01-18

"1517" 1-01-18

"Click, Click" 1-16-18

"Unhooked" 12-08-17

"Come Back Soon" 8-22-17

"Slow Motion" 8-18-17

"Turning" 12-02-17

"Mazed" 11-21-17

"Subtle Feels" 11-28-17

"Premium" 11-25-17

"January Flakes" 1-16-18

"The One Who Got Away" 9-18-17

"Summer Flung" 11-14-17

"Yet" 11-17-17

"Recently Self-Directed" 8-23-17

"Contracting Works" 8-23-17

"Still Awake" 6-28-17

"Ajar" 6-28-17

"Sugar Rot" 7-14-17

"In Grades" 6-28-17

"Showered" 7-10-17

"Life After" 4-09-17

"Bad News" 12-07-17

"W17" 12-08-17

"Ha" 12-20-17

"Shiver" 12-17-17

"Reflection" 11-06-17

"Even Again" 11-09-17

"Into Me You See" 12-08-17

"Out of Sync" 1-13-18

"Kckrrksssk" 1-01-18

"Shake My Head" 1-04-18

"Sightline" 1-10-18

"Ash Blows Away" 1-16-18

"Dried Up" 1-16-18

"Precious Memory" 1-06-18

"First Impressions Updated" 1-18-18

"Forward Motion" 1-16-18

"Forward Motion Too" 1-16-18

"Hands Up" 1-07-18

"Technicolor" 1-17-18

"Design" 1-16-18

"Impetus" 1-15-18

"Ahhhhh" 12-18-17

"Reverse-Engineer" 1-21-18

"Naturally" 12-08-17

//

About The Author:

Hillary Kaitlyn Walsh was born on October 17, 1991 in Maryland *(hint so you can figure out ages and timelines for poems)*. She enjoys writing poems and short stories on the side, and dreams of publishing short stories in addition to her poems. She has a "sweet and sour combo" of 2 rescue female black cats named Kettle and Rose. Hillary currently works as a contractor serving and supporting adults with intellectual and developmental disabilities. She reads an average of one book per week to learn and grow. Hillary plans to earn a master's degree in social work and continue her education to receive an LCSW-C in order to counsel adults and youth, specifically those struggling with mental illness and charting personal growth. Sales of this book help her save money to achieve that dream. Hillary has planted a few of her books in free book libraries for fun with special messages. Please support your free book libraries! Books instill greater knowledge and sensitivity.

Contact her at hillarykwalsh@gmail.com or follow @HillaryKaitlyn on Instagram and "Hillary Kaitlyn Walsh" YouTube. Hillary reads some of her poetry on her YouTube and provides some context. Hillary is available for booking at events and is excited to champion writing, communication, empowerment, and more.

\\

2018

Jen! 2016